KITTENS

FOR WHEN SH*T HAPPENS...

To Frazzle and Pringle, my own 'go to' cats...
... oh, and Caren – my wife.

An Hachette UK Company
www.hachette.co.uk

First published in Great Britain in 2013 by
Spruce, a division of Octopus Publishing Group Ltd
Endeavour House
189 Shaftesbury Avenue
London
WC2H 8JY
www.octopusbooks.co.uk
www.octopusbooksusa.com

Copyright © Octopus Publishing Group Ltd 2013

Distributed in the US by
Hachette Book Group USA
237 Park Avenue
New York NY 10017 USA

Distributed in Canada by
Canadian Manda Group
165 Dufferin Street
Toronto, Ontario, Canada M6K 3H6

Trevor Davies asserts the moral right to be identified as the author of this work

ISBN 978-1-84601-417-8

A CIP catalogue record for this book is available from the British Library

Printed and bound in China

2 4 6 8 10 9 7 5 3 1

KITTENS

FOR WHEN SH*T HAPPENS...

spruce

Trevor Davies

CONTENTS

INTRODUCTION

It is a fact universally acknowledged that no problem seems as big when faced with a kitten by your side. The palliative effect of young felines has long been known in medical circles and kittens are regularly used in operating theatres to distract patients when no general anaesthetic is available. That is why it occurred to the publishers that an essential first aid manual with a kitten for everyday emergencies was a public service that couldn't be overlooked.

How to use this book

1. **Locate your specific emergency on the contents page.**
2. **Turn the pages until you find the appropriate kitten.**
3. **Feel your troubles disappear*.**

Please note, the emergencies for which we've provided cats are those that are more emotional than physical: affairs of the heart or work-related stress, for example. If you've picked up this book because you've fallen off your bike and broken your collarbone, or you're simply on fire, please put the book down and phone the relevant emergency service. There's only so much a kitten can do.

However, if you've just split up from a partner or are feeling physically inadequate, then you're in the right place.

Disclaimers

Should you read this book and still feel stressed, consult your doctor, therapist or bookstore (it could be that you're in need of a puppy rather than a kitten, in which case you need *Puppies For When Sh*t Happens*, conveniently published by the same people).

Lastly, no kittens were badly harmed in the making of this book. Some were slightly bruised and a few walked out because of the lack of blue M&Ms in their trailers, but we had plenty of back-ups.

*Adult dosage – no more than two kittens per day, always read the collar.

Home
emergencies

Although she'd only ironed one sock, Veronica decided it was time for a nap.

Bored with chores?

Initially, Ray was pleased with his plan to save money on the kids' airfares by packing them up for the removal men. It was only when things went ominously quiet that he realized he'd forgotten to make air holes.

Moving home?

To his horror, Barnaby realized that in planting his runner beans at the bottom of the garden he had unwittingly dug up his mother's remains.

Hopeless gardener?

Feonella stopped immediately when she saw a hair in her cookie dough. It was ginger and curly.

Culinary failure?

Annoying flatmate?

Broken something?

No money?

This was the one place Smokey could get some respite from the nagging to finish the decorating.

DIY disaster?

Day-to-day
travails

Bad hair day?

All Mr Chuckles had to do was wait. He knew that any moment a precocious claret with a cheeky bouquet was coming his way.

Need a drink?

It wasn't the beer, the riotous singing or the 3 a.m. burger that had made Widget feel ill. It was the fact that he couldn't recall anything about his grandmother's funeral.

Hungover?

Weather woes?

From the way people were staring, Zebedee wondered whether he might have something on his bottom lip.

Fashion faux pas?

Best intentions failed?

Like most things he attempted, tree-climbing wasn't turning out quite the way Duncan had hoped.

Why did I do that?

Wrong place, wrong time?

Twizzle's response to the suggestion of some worming tablets was a touch rude, but not unexpected.

Got out of bed on the wrong side?

At 4 a.m., and after ten minutes of not blinking, Russell regretted his midnight snack of double espresso and amphetamines.

Insomnia?

Eleanor was finally considering buying a smaller car. This was the fifth time she'd failed her test because she wasn't able to reach either the pedals or the steering wheel.

Failed driving test?

Ed decided to cut out the middleman.

Over-indulged?

Wish you hadn't started something?

Karaoke disaster?

It may have contained three times the recommended calories; it may have ended her diet after only two days, but that full-fat budgie was delicious.

Just can't help yourself?

Priscilla thought adding the pearls might be too showy for a parent–teacher meeting.

Trying too hard?

Although the others weren't saying anything, they were all thinking the same thing. Either Pascal's new piece entitled 'Space' was ground-breaking conceptual art, or he was taking the piss.

Misunderstood?

Never learn from your mistakes?

Work
worries

Commuting hell?

Terry's boss hadn't taken the news of the stationery order error too well.

Boss hates you?

Bullied at work?

Stuck in a dead-end job?

The photographer's request for 'more ferocity, less ears' was met with a degree of confusion, but mainly contempt.

Unfair expectations?

Leonard had no idea how he was going to finish this report by 5 p.m. as he still had to knock over the houseplants, spread litter all over the kitchen floor and pee behind the television.

Looming deadlines?

Struggling to face up to your responsibilities?

Dealing with idiots?

It was clear that the only way her husband would get off his arse was if Saffy catapulted it into next-door's tree.

Lack motivation?

Need a pay rise?

Ten minutes into his revision Brian suffered a calamitous apathy attack.

Can't concentrate?

Her husband, kids and work colleagues all knew she was a bitch before her third cup.

Not enough coffee?

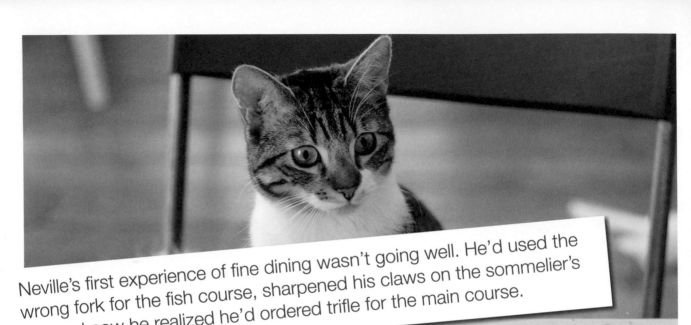

Neville's first experience of fine dining wasn't going well. He'd used the wrong fork for the fish course, sharpened his claws on the sommelier's leg, and now he realized he'd ordered trifle for the main course.

Out of your depth?

Frazzle could neither beat the bastards nor join them, so she retired to her box.

On the brink of a nervous breakdown?

On reflection, Frosty should have practised before inviting everyone to watch her 'high dive into the water bowl'.

Difficulty getting noticed?

After spending yesterday dressed as a giant cheese, Basil was determined that today's disguise would be a success.

Constant failure?

Relationship problems

Bubbles still couldn't understand how this could possibly be man's best friend.

Tiresome companion?

Norman's confession not only ended their relationship, but also explained the burning sensation Pringle experienced every time she peed.

Bad break-up?

Annoying neighbours?

Let's get this straight, I'm not your little fluffykins; I only sit on your lap because the house is so fucking cold and after every unsolicited hug I do a small wee in your sock drawer.

Taken for granted?

Pete had thought his date was going swimmingly. It wasn't until Miss Biggles invited him back to her hutch for a carrot that he realized his mistake.

Always pick the wrong person?

Ironically, while Leonard was getting citrus fruits with biscuity high notes, it was Tiffy who was getting the arsehole.

Unwanted attention?

Camilla had lain there for two hours, too scared to turn around and find out whom she had brought home from the office party. Now the full horror of what she'd done was in her face... It was George from Accounts!

Persistent offender?

Feeling lonely?

After her third break-up in two months,
Miffy just needed a hug... from anyone.

Unlucky in love?

Misread the situation?

Confidence issues?

Still hold a candle?

Alphonse had been feeling slightly ostracized from the gang ever since he'd described their bandana as 'cerise'.

Feel like you don't belong?

It was another brilliant hiding place and Raffles never knew what had hit him!

People find you irritating?

Family frustrations

Snowflake was convinced he was adopted.

Family feud?

Tomorrow the kids would fight over the PlayStation; her husband would drink too much and insult her mother; and she'd probably burn the turkey and be disappointed with her presents, but Holly couldn't help herself... she adored Christmas.

Seasonal stress?

Naughty kids?

Loretta awoke from dreams of last night's fling with the Spanish waiter to find herself sunburnt and with a worrying itch.

Bad holiday?

Annoying siblings?

Embarrassing parents?

Age, health
and hope

The terrifying truth was beginning to dawn on Jasper. He was allergic to cats.

Health problems?

Skye had dropped a lot of acid in the 70s, but her flashbacks were as vivid today as they ever were.

Feel old?

Memory failing?

No energy?

When Humphrey spotted the Blue-Hat Cats he sent in his new wingman.

Growing pains?

Agnes approached her new breakfast multi-vitamin diet drink with the expectation of it not tasting as good as her normal bacon sandwich.

Starting a diet?

Diet depression?

Although quarterback was always considered the coolest position, Ziggy was simply fed up with staring at Paul's arse.

Sporting failure?

Keith was surprised to find that it wasn't a hairball after all.

Eaten something you shouldn't have?

Physically inadequate?

Noodle was beginning to think that, either she'd gone too far this time, or the fireman was going to need a longer ladder.

In serious trouble?

Hooter's trampoline practice was going well and soon both the bird table and the shelf of ornaments would be back in reach.

Not as mobile as you used to be?

Parker suspected that the other cats' compliments on his new hat lacked a certain veracity.

The butt of the joke?

Feeling unattractive?